NIGHT SONG

The fourth selection of nineteen poems by the finest poetical voice of the post-war generation of English poets. Including 'Grass' finished when Shänne Sands was only eighteen.

'Thank you ... for those sweet words of poetry which touched me deeply.'
HRH, The Maharajah of Bundi (1956)

Shänne Sands

Further selections of poems by Shänne Sands

Vol.1   Fidelity Is For Swans
Vol.2   The Silver Hooves
Vol.3   Moonlight On Words
Vol.5   Fragments Of Desire

NIGHT SONG

Selected Poems By
SHÄNNE SANDS

Volume 4

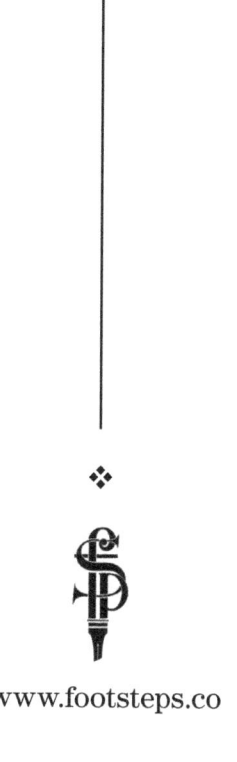

www.footsteps.co

© Shänne Sands 2012

The right of Shänne Sands to be identified as the author of this work and illustrations has been asserted in accordance with sections 77 and 78 of the copyright designs and patents act 1988.

Night Song

Footsteps Press first edition
www.footsteps.co

Cover design by Kevin Reilly and
Jackie Pascoe

Typeset by Jackie Pascoe

Set in century
ISBN 978-0-9566349-9-3

Reproduction of any or all of this work in any form, electronic or otherwise, is expressly forbidden without the prior contractual agreement of the author. Incidental illustrations are taken from the original hand written volumes by Shänne Sands.

To my Phoebe and Sophie,
two wonderful aunts who
believed in miracles

Incidental illustrations from the original hand written scripts

POEMS

Grass	1
Somebody Asked Me	7
The Return Of Words	9
Unseen	11
Innocence	12
Being In Love	13
The Jew	14
We Change	15
Looe '65	19
I Want To Cry	20
Springfields	21
... And So I Weep	22
Come And See	24
The Kiss	26
Poor John Clare	27
Sonnet	28
Rejoice	29
Between The Sheets	30
An Epilogue (Grass)	31

Grass

I

Shall we move on -
As the dry, dying grass moves on with the wind.
To where only the last living particle can follow
Before or after all,
Which brings only emptiness of mind and soul,
Which even great Plato could not master -
On with the dying grass -
Moving faster and then faster.
　　　　　　Always still -
Yet in the stillness of the moving wind
And dry, dying grass -
Life breaks away and seeds fall and damage their skins
Upon the callous earth -
The earth desperate for life,
Yields only that which must grow deformed and die,
From its beauty into dry ugliness of shape.
This intercourse of life and death speaks of waste.
Too many great minds have suffered -
Too many small minds have thrived
On a dead man's curse.
　　　　　　Let us move -
Escape with the now decayed grass,
On, on to find the right conception of that,
Of which we know so little.

II

　　　　　　Let us move on -
To where the long field ends -
To where the colour of the grass fades
From stubborn green to blue.
White blue grass with tints of whitish gold
Made beautiful from the ochre of the sun.

III

　　　　　　Beyond the colour-changing grass
I try to find in desperation the truth of learning -
The truth of experience,
But I find only age weary at my side

Weary as myself is weary of all this learning.

IV

                Nothing is still or dead
All is moving.
A whole moving world.
We cannot hope to become a part of that
Of which we already are,
We can only move on with the grass,
The dry, dying grass,
On with the wind and slow October rains -
                Moving not with the leaves but over the leaves.
                Moving and living because of the leaves.
We must not hope, yet we do hope
And because we hope
We pray.
With the mountain and the lake our thoughts reflect
Just as with the grass our hair tangles
Just as with the wind our thoughts smile.
                Nothing is still or dead
All is moving.
Every movement calls the singing nearer -
Until a world breaks from a world
And becomes a truthful master.
                Faster and faster now the colours turn,
Blue upon blue - every colour turning.
Moving with the grass towards
The mighty voice of singing.

V

                And then silence -
                Except for the burning of coal -
And little beads of perspiration in your ears.
Must the answer always be so like the blunt edge
Of a sticky knife
Must the key always be left
In someone else's purse,
And the words fall from the tongue of the man,
Who brings only regret.
Must we all clap our hands

When the play has just begun to have a meaning -
After learning so much - to find so little.
Then amidst it all -
The grass awaits to change its colour
For perhaps who - we wonder - how we wonder.
Station after station passes on
Only to find one a stranger,
Having Sunday tea in a dress with no sleeves
Conversation is not true.
Books we find only breed conceit.
Wait for the grass
Wait for the sun to burn your life
Into the battle of reality -
And the conquering of a spiritual blessing.
Wait for the water to drop into your throat
The healing moisture from love
Love from water into grass.
Grass 'round your throat -
Grass touching and holding the true sounds,
The look from our eyes can pass between
One mysterious wave of light.
Oh! The knots we tie!
The narrow red cuts in the back,
Where the bone holds only skin,
Loose skin and nails that break
Breaking away from the very sleep we shelter in.
We grow tired of waiting for the grass.
     Grass -
The agony of waiting
The agony of pity
The agony of hope

VI

    Does it seem very faraway the top of the hill?
We only live to forget that which we cannot hope
To understand,
We only live to forget.
We shall find failure in reaching for the grass
For we must not yet understand,
But we may turn with the grass
For we may turn with the grass
All the colours of a rainbow upon the ground.

Now has all the past turned to find a new beginning
Now all is moving with the wind -
        Shall we move on -
Long roots hold so many back, long roots of grass.
Now is all prepared for time's shadow
To follow and cause alarm -
Even time could not leave the shadow -
The shadow we all must carry,
To and from this apology of existence.
This case or cage of crystallized memories of doubt.
Only to die as ignorant as we were born -
        Shall we move on
As the dry, dying grass moves on with the wind
To where the new spring may still rejoice
And capture new laughter
From the once silent woods of fond stillness.

VII

        We who are moving
To find a new-self
A new expression of that which we know so well.
Moving as thoughts move
Thought and movement of self
Only to make a more complex anxiety
Of one's own personality.
Only to free oneself from a butchered theory
Into a more helpless point of view
        And still we shall move with the grass.
Moving because of the grass
Fearing as we enter the realms of our new discovery.
        Nothing is still or dead -
        All is moving -
The closing doors always
Leave behind a movement of air,
The vacuum of the found or lost.
And with all the ignorance shall we still find sincerity
Enough to learn a little wisdom.
Not all can come from one straight line -
Not all can be surrounded by a circle -
Time will appear only to be a Scaramouche,
But even Time must do penance.
As even grass must move and turn the many colours -

Until all vapidity has indeed vanished.
                        The spirit of the grass shall return -
With the living sorrow of a past world
The greatness of music
The humility in one single drop of rain -

VIII

I have since moved in a crowd with the moving world
Where the rain and the sun shared
The honour of serving such as these.
We who have known delight in other joys -
Will have little to tell but so much to carry us forth
Towards the very smallest grain of hope,
Even when the end of all beginnings shakes our hands,
We who are filled with the newness of a bright-coin,
Shall sing.

IX

If only we had been prepared to unfold this symbol
Without pain
We are told to feel
This perpetual movement of the moving grass
                        Shall we move on -
Move on -- move on --
Let us go to the very first.
Let us pretend.
Only we find there is no pretending
Only dry, dying grass for even grass must die
Let us move on to where the long field ends.
To where the colour of the grass fades
From stubborn green to blue.
All is green, nay all is blue.
Is there no answer?
I beg for those who suffer
I beg for my soul.
We cannot find the answer -
And I am too small to find an answer -

X

                      Yet still there is joy
Listen you shall hear-
'Come unto me and be healed' ,
We cannot find this answer
This searching has numbed the very existence
Of all we understand.
                      Nothing is everything -
And all shall be part of the essence of all that ever was.
Because this was meant to be -
And all and so much more
Will find the grass waiting for the wind.
The wind longing for the grass
All shall be cleansed with this new found longing -
Cleansed with this everlasting pattern of movement.
For moving is to be aching with pain -
Joyful with tears
Brimming with the knowledge that we are all lost.
Utterly, completely, lost.
And in the losing we are saved.
Our very bodies shall not fall
But move on with the grass
                      Never, never shall this be said again.
For the answer shall come like the finding of a pearl
So filled with the colour of prayer -
                      And now the miracle has happened.

Somebody Asked Me

Somebody asked me
The other day about you, saying
With that knowing look in their dim eyes,
'You can't still love him
After everything that's happened'
My thoughts left the conversation and went ahead -
Could they really know 'everything' that happened -
Oh not the quick insult
Or the vapid lie -
Or the 'others'' taken in a fit of sex -
Or the endless separation built
On my calendar like huge ugly steps
Higher and higher into my life -
No they didn't have a clue
About what really happened -

How one day in April '61 in England -
By the Thames -
From some obscure patch of darkness
You came into my life -
A torch flared not easy to put out -
When our bodies touched
That same torch, became
A dazzle cast about our bed -

How the back of your head slightly bent
Moved me beyond words -
Or how your sour face
Cross or tired suddenly made me chuckle -
How in a fit of white-hot love
You'd strip me bare and throw
My body across a fitted carpet -
Better than any mattress on the pretty bed.

Could they know how we laughed
At life's grim 'handouts', because our
Love was massive in a small untidy
World of petty shadows -
And that my heart could carry
Your soul along every problem,
Every sad mistake -
Because we had sung a song my love,
Across a wooden table; piled with
Plates and flowers turned to a fable

That was us.
And when they ask me silly questions
I want to yell,
'What do you know of love?'
But I turn my head away
And slowly think of you -
And wonder in this rather lonely minute
If you remember April '61 and that river too!

The Return Of Words

I had forgotten
Poetry is but words
Love, but kisses
Death, but a going cold
Of both.

I should have remembered -
Not allowed my emotions
To come to a standstill
On a damp day,
In some unwelcome town -

I should have lived -
A hundred words a minute -
And kissed you into a frenzy -
Long before death got in the way

Got in the way -
Of little rainbows
After slight showers
After green fields lost in mist
And after supper when it's nearly dark -

I should have broken this curse
Of silence thro' my mind -
Opened-up my brain and let in some light -
But almost before I was aware of Time
It had escaped -
Time had fled and I was
Wordless, kissless, and I saw death
Coldly lying in a 'Rest-house' -

Now words return -
Slowly, love, ah, such a
Heaven to hope for may
Open me up again -
I am not completely slain -
Way back in a dim corner of myself
Poetry is singing -

Words are ready for rehearsal
Away cold death -
Away feeble emotions -
Away you thousand torments of the bone -

I am capable again
To laugh and think -
Write and feel -
I've broken a spell
Of torture -
My brain is a mass of unwritten words
All laced with kisses, wine and friends -

Find me a pen -
Some paper -
And a second -

I shall leave you verses
To speak aloud - to shout from baths -
To quote above all havoc's wreck -
To weep to and to dance -
Poetry is but words and words are free.
Run through the fields -
Fly, fly after me.

The Unseen

Here, unseen
My words fade into air,
Falling with autumn leaves -
Birds peck at their edges -
People walk over my words
Careless of what could be
Under their feet -

Nobody, not even I,
Speak the fallen words
Aloud, strangely the woods
Echo their meaning
Almost by love -

My words fall into rivers,
Where water-spirits sleep
Upon them, where small fish
Try to eat them -
My words swim with the ripple
Of cool streams -
Yellow irises protect them,

Unseen, here
My words mark their destiny -

Innocence

Our innocence was kept in a blue vase -
Holding chrysanthemums with heavy heads -
Or over gas fires making toast and reading Flecker
Or lying on narrow beds comfortable with happiness -
Books littered with petals and 'notes'
About coming 'home' late -
Piping a recorder in the dusk of that autumn,
When words spun to the ground with united pleasure -
Only the flowers fell one by one -
The words were never weak -
Only the autumn's changed from then till now;
As vases hold other flowers and our innocence
Is no longer found within their blueness
On a high mantelpiece,
But is a piece of jagged glass
Broken yet still beautiful -

Being In Love

A touch of skin, the smell of shampoo'd hair -
Teeth and toes, nails, soft backs even shadows -
The laughter in bed,
Just being there -
The big rows, little fights, tears and smiles
Desolate parting –
Endless longing -
Every breathing second thinking of him -
The passion blind –
The passion strong -
Dozens of kisses caught between dreams -
Always right –
Never wrong -
Heaven for the young -
A glow of youth for age,
Letters, gifts, poems, songs -
Music, wine and dance -
Never too late or too soon -
Always adored like spring sunshine -
And a long stemmed-rose in a sweet girl's room -
The broken-heart dying in a diamond cage -
As memories throb -
One emotion shared by rich and poor -
Lovers cuff-links -
His words -
The loving of another -
Giving of yourself -
The soul's jacket amid yellow roses -
A now and always of perfect wealth

The Jew

Above-our heads is the divine presence of God,
Yet we walk a twisted path far from the shores
Where the sand took our messages -
And we kept our temples clean -
We are hated in many tongues
And cursed from generation to generation -

Yet we still rock to and fro muttering
The prayers of Abraham our father -
Long ago our tents became fine houses in new lands -
Some of us exchanged this luxury for German
Concentration-camps;
The gas-ovens and the bullet by a waiting-grave -
Others fought to erect once more
The blue and white flag,
David's flag,
Beside the hills and rocks,
Where the Maccabaeus shone their noble swords -

We drift now only as they drift who are weary,
Yet not too tired to weep and we weep
For many who will not weep again!
And with the divine presence of God above out heads
We chant our prayers and linger
In countries, where tomorrow may strike us down!

We Change

We change -
Not with colour of skin
Or plastic surgery, but with
An inner feeling that we are different -
Able to think back along a line of years,
When there came certain thoughts -
We could only suffer in thought -
But finding the first pain
Was a cut belly, we knew agony
On a hospital bed, where there
Have been dead more grim from pain
Than even war gives pictures of!

Living on we found
The 'Hellos' of strangers were not prayers
To be said before meals, but only
Hello's the word we use before
The final goodbye.

After ten years a thin line
Spoiled a perfect forehead -
The changing face lost some youth
And held every tooth to prove
Something could be kept without too
Much damage to the body -
What of the spirit?
Hitched-up inside a flat chest -
Or the soul kept underfoot
By a frightened Homosapien -
Can this find expression
Take flight into thin air,
Where 'fall-outs' might catch
An unsuspecting soul -
Even souls decay between
The green hedges -

We delve, not too deeply -
This would cause lack of sleep
In some even madness -
And we'd be irritable in the morning
Of all our memories -

We caress and kiss our ghosts -
Who played havoc

With a broken heart -
And then depart
Not too quickly, so that you may catch
One last glimpse of love
Then watch it fade away -
On the face of a travelling clock -
We stop -
Abruptly, we dare not move -
The rent-man will think we're out -
And stop knocking -
Then we shout -
'All great bores were tolerant you know'
But great men are wild (and some women)
Their most peaceful handshake
Is the wildness that puts things right -

We change -
Keeping only the first look
Of birth in our eyes -
The constant surprise that living
We are born to die -
And dying we are meant to live again -
Of course the intellectual arguments are insane -
Of course, of course -

On the lap of forest creatures
Collecting food for a harsh winter -
You will find fur - soft with encouragement
To keep guts warm -
But our guts are covered with skin -
That swells in old age
And eats itself sick -
We over-eat and feasting devours
Countries even worlds
With a tick from the travelling clock -

The barking dogs fight their foe
With such loud barks
They're glad to go
And find another bone -
'Its mine'
'Its mine'
'Its mine'
A splintered bone remains

Stripped of meat -
The dogs retreat -
And a red poppy sticks out of the
Dead bone's head!

The price of love is to stay the same -
Well, we change -
And lose a family and Saturday tea
In their contemporary flat -
We are self, able to explore
The situations on a sea-shore
Far from home -
Where listening to shells
We hear the chimes of a loved city -
The smallness of it all could never matter -
Only that it seemed so huge,
Before we left -
Huge with pregnant hope -
That burnt your heart -
Into all this smallness -

Only the white tears as they
Fall off our chin -
Only the voice of mothers
Calling their children in -

Poetry be the salvation
For a tired arm -
Words more lovely that a girl
Words more wanted that a fella -
Words play on the tongue
Better than water -
Words of poetry spoken not by the poets
But their ink -
The man may stink with vice
But his poetry ah, his poetry ...
Made you forget the hour,
When sleep wouldn't come -
It bridged the gap you thought
You understood -
And soothed a brain to rest -

We change
We grow-up -

We grow old -
We grow down,
We weary and we frown -

Nothing is too much to bear -
Only perhaps the greying of our hair -
To see a dimple on a baby's knee,
Is more than age can ever be -

Staring into all the fairy rings
Disturbing the letters on the mat -
Thinking of spacemen
And how elder statesmen die -
And why the street is full of passers-by -
The crowd, always in thousands
Cheering at kings and queens -
Watching workmen put a city up -
Still there when its pulled down -
The crowd -
The passer-by -
Its safe on cement -
You can be content!

Eden will grow again -
The apple will be lost -

We change -
We grumble -
But in ourselves
We might have been -
A crust of something
Fresh and new and clean!

Looe '65

Across the flagstones, pink and grey
Stretch another sea-breeze day -

Sleepy-eyed I dressed
Then ate, then went

Into the wind-bent town -
Shopped around

For fruit and veg
4d stamps and hyacinths -

Little boats jogged up and down -
As my hair blew wild -

High-up a sky so clear - so blue
Down here flagstones pink and grey

Lie rain-splashed, moon-marked - old -
Near me a Cornish field - a blue-stained sea.

I Want To Cry

I want to cry, but I can't
I want to exhaust my body
Not with copulation, but with tears -
But I can only shed loose hairs
Tears do not fall easily anymore -

My emotions are stiff doors
Shut tightly - pushing against them
May break them open -
Push against me, my love,
Break me apart - open me -
Let me cry for both of us -
Tears for years -
For our moments,
For booze and friends
Books and trains
A box at Covent-Garden
Then a splendid row -
Push against me with your shoulders -
I am a stiff door -
Open me, my love -
For love's sake make me cry -
Then, O then comfort me!

SPRINGFIELDS
           (NORTH DEVON)

How quiet this room -
Untouched by anyone -
Late afternoon -

The washing line outside
Sways to and fro -
Wide, wide, wide -

Flowers' lovely heads -
A thousand petals fall -
All brightest red

Soft is this grass -
And perfect this earth -
As insects pass

Across everything
That grows and dies
And lives again next spring -

For now
This room moving
With some sweet power -

Holds me quiet and free -
Warmed through with sun -
To stand and gaze and be.

... And So I Weep

And so I weep
Not tears they are meek -
My grief is hard like bones -
And filled-up with life's moans -
My weeping is a lost day -
Buried and loved and passed away.

My weeping is for all we lost -
The dead-years - the sunsets we tossed
Into the seas out of our reach
Forever like a holiday beach.

Becoming only a snap-shot in my mind -
Remembering a hot summer-afternoon,
Sealed and signed for loving -
Fair and free
You and me
All sand and sea -

With a breeze blowing around -
A cloak spread on the ground
My weeping could be walked upon
Until the storm had gone -

Had gone over the hill's back
The highest hill in the black
Country-side of lost ideals,
Where to exist means not to feel -

Not to feel joy or quick pain -
Not to feel love or to know that rain
Can be soft and warm and sweet -
To taste, to touch and will beat

Against a breast like a lover
Beating against a heart - to discover
Another world growing near a rose
Or pink petals over my toes.

And so I weep -
Not tears they are meek -
But great pieces of yesterday's keep-sakes
That float over a lake of desire and heart-break

Floating over my destiny
Hiding away from me a key
That will turn locks of so-called-sin
To gold-dust and let me begin -

Let me begin again -
Like buckets of new grain
Ready to grow and survive -
Waiting to come alive!

Come And See

Come and see
Come and see
The roads are pushing our fields away -

Today
Today -
Come and see
The decay
Of the city.

Come and see
The social security see-saw -
Human-apes
Stupidity plus stupidity -

Come and see
Our broken down economy
Rather old policies
Balance of payments
Not achieved, cheer, cheer
And try to explain inflation -
Come and see
Come and hear!

The failed master plan -
The behaviour pattern
Of aged ministers of State -
Too late
Too late -

Sing the song of the out-of-work
The three day week
The endless rain -
A country going down the drain -

But tighten your seat-belts -
Switch on your colour TV

And to the hounds
With wages and prices -
All clap hands
For the 'Common-Market'
And pick your nose
When no-one is looking -

Come and see
The decay of a country -
Export the flag -
And try again -
More rain
More roads -

Surprise, surprise -
Academic exercise
Stretches the mind -
But recognise
In time
Sales for the home-market
Has to shake hands
With the people!

The Kiss

I caught your kiss
In a silver spoon
Saw myself upside down,
An image in a moon-like dish.

I mounted your kiss
In a shank of golden glass -
Wore it for a ring where
It sang on my small finger

Suddenly it became a butterfly
All pale yellow, deep blue, soft mauve
And it flew across my heart
Leaving wet gloss marks for tears.

Poor John Clare

Poor John Clare -
'I think I see him seated in his chair'
The way a poet sits -
As words sang their morning-song
Thro' his country mind -
But did such words prove too unkind -
Cheerless and cruel -
Did madness tempt him away from happiness?
As poetry kept his tender heart in pain
What dreadful influence danced beneath
The gay good-will of John Clare's brain!

Covered with feathers shaken from the birds
High in the trees that held your words -
You tamed the winter robin to your hand -
But could not tame the madness around your eyes -
Nor could you understand how those you loved
Sent you away from fields your boyhood knew
And locked-up your spirit behind a leafless wall -
And called you mad-disgraced and devil-filled!

Poor John Clare
'I think I see him seated in his chair'
Speaking softly to a small brown hen -
With a note of pity in all his singing lines -
Poetry was his evening talk and in the
Slow step of his walk, when insane
Loneliness and poverty drove him to tears
Thoughts and actions went against
The domestic pattern of his cottage life -
The Asylum took his afflicted mind and bound
His freedom to stake, where he died -

Sonnet

If I could control the deepest love-magic -
With incantations rare, profound, true and proud -
I with love's wand would wave away all tragic
Happenings and with love's spell shout sweet yet loud
Such promises of faith to make you again strong,
Young, beautiful in face, soul, word and power -
Forever to claim that everlasting place and belong
In limb, brain, heart, eyes to my flower
Of love's own rose petals; perfect to see,
A song-filled pulse, to Earth's own given.
You would at last walk towards me
At last with magic-spirit stand forgiven.

Yet in this living second, I remember
I cannot magic May into grey December.

Rejoice

Rejoice the rain -
Familiar scenes will not come again,
As comes the thunderbolt
Thro' the storm -
As grips the eagle to its prey
As sacred goats, bulls, cows
Are led away -
Youth's immense sorrows,
Immense joys will not come again.

Rejoice the oak -
Even Olympian gods voiced
Their praise, downwards
To the mighty roots -
As mountains shone and
Latin poets sacrificed words
To Zeus -

Rejoice the olive -
A wreath for those who chose glory even
Before heaven -
Yet that simple fruit
Gives not a food in years.
And the oil covers ancient tears -
As an embrace -

Rejoice the dove -
The special love of those whose fruit
Is peace - Ah! Why
The dreaded stones of hate,
When gentle doves guard
The city gates.

Rejoice the purest air -
Finding there always the liberated souls
Of those who take for their own,
A wrapped cloth of life -
Holding deep within
Its lilac folds
The hundred promises
Of life, the gold of
Rain, oak, olive, dove.

Between Two Sheets

Between two sheets
We love each other
With a passion excitingly
Like electric strings -
Full of unique surprise
Suddenly the blue of your eyes
Near my own
And my reflection,
Hot with desire
And healthy lust -
Your body a lyric swinging
Back and forth highlighting
My back and arms and my face
With light

An Epilogue (Grass)

After the miracle we moved
Into the moving ground -
Our nerves were jagged
With lost air and everything
Of which we became a part
Left us only drained
Of all we hoped to find -
Many were the hopes we left behind -
And leaving dead leaves above
The ground, drifting towards
The eaters of dreams, where
Screams uncaged and free -
Made their own humanity -
Miseries painted gold
Almost seemed fulfilled -
And waiting figures held their arms
Across the window-sills -

Subconscious is the world
Behind the stairs -
Where all is black-out
And faint whispers -
The very least is born to pavements -
The most to gold -
And between the lost creation -
The individual free and wild
Fills in the moments
With immortal interpreters who glide
And stare around the dead leaves -
And falling skin -
Where age has touched the pebbles
And let the water in -

We meet the image -
Say our prayers -
Drive the nails into painted doors -
Then weep and shudder
On floors we almost forgot
To clean!

Language helps the situation -
As we act words into place and person.
But silence has a serious tread -
Yet we follow, follow, follow -

Solemn in our demonstration -
Leaving only fire burning, burning,
Burning all desire -
Desireless we sit beneath great tree-roots
Under the earth; feeling almost new-birth -
But we do not want to be born again -
We are part of the miracle -
Inside the pearl -
And birth with bricks with dirt -
With claws with vines -
Is the terrible-beautiful we left behind -

Events made living quite impossible -
Here among the roots spun warm
With earth - wounds feel soft
And blood is free from argument -
Complete surrender to the moving
Difference of this new world,
Where a familiar frost nips
Your finger-tips into their new strangeness
And we suddenly remember how sad
It was to be mistaken -
So we awaken -
With a purity almost unbearable -
Like perfect music listen to
And understood -
Knowing that tree roots are also wood -
Voices chanting with the moving madness
Strange and blind -
Only voices could be so unkind -
Cruel dark sounds invade the miracle
We found -

And we are buried beneath
The moving ground -
Desireless, twisted with roots
We become stiff and cold -
Slowly dust which is also cruel
Drifts back high on the moving ground.
Searching once again for everything
We never found -

Into all the air and blowing winds -
Dust all alone shakes

Onto every movement -
Then of course we know
From this beginning flowers grow -
And into the consciousness of words
Life itself sings with the birds -
And softly, softly, softly back and forth
The moving ground sensitive with tears
Takes our nothingness and fears
Into itself so that we live
Again, again, again -
And living rejoice with lambs
In spring along the echo
Of our songs.

www.ingramcontent.com/pod-product-compliance
Lightning Source LLC
Chambersburg PA
CBHW051720040426
42446CB00008B/976